W9-AWW-318

HUMAN FACTORS IN ENGINEERING AND DESIGN

HUMAN FACTORS IN ENGINEERING AND DESIGN

SEVENTH EDITION

Mark S. Sanders, Ph.D.

California State University, Northridge

Ernest J. McCormick, Ph.D.

Late Professor Emeritus of Psychological Sciences,
Purdue University

McGraw-Hill, Inc.
New York St. Louis San Francisco Auckland Bogotá
Caracas Lisbon London Madrid Mexico City Milan
Montreal New Delhi San Juan Singapore
Sydney Tokyo Toronto

This book is printed on acid-free paper.

HUMAN FACTORS IN ENGINEERING AND DESIGN

Copyright © 1993, 1987, 1982, 1976 by McGraw-Hill, Inc. All rights reserved. Previously published under the following titles: *Human Factors Engineering,* copyright © 1970, 1964 by McGraw-Hill, Inc., all rights reserved; and *Human Engineering,* copyright © 1957 by McGraw-Hill, Inc., all rights reserved. Printed in the United States of America. Except as permitted under the United States Copyright Act of 1976, no part of this publication may be reproduced or distributed in any form or by any means, or stored in a data base or retrieval system, without the prior written permission of the publisher.

0 DOC DOC 9 0 9

ISBN 0-07-054901-X

This book was set in Times Roman by Better Graphics, Inc.
The editors were Christopher Rogers and Tom Holton;
the production supervisor was Denise L. Puryear.
The cover was designed by Carla Bauer.
R. R. Donnelley & Sons Company was printer and binder.

Library of Congress Cataloging-in-Publication Data

Sanders, Mark S.
    Human factors in engineering and design / Mark S. Sanders, Ernest
J. McCormick.—7th ed.
       p.   cm.
    Includes bibliographical references and index.
    ISBN 0-07-054901-X
    1. Human engineering.   I. McCormick, Ernest J. (Ernest James)
II. Title.
TA166.S33   1993
620.8'2—dc20   92-194

ABOUT THE AUTHORS

DR. MARK S. SANDERS received his M.S. and Ph.D. degrees in human factors from Purdue University. He is currently Professor and Chair of the Human Factors Applied Experimental Psychology Graduate Program at California State University, Northridge. Also Dr. Sanders consults with various organizations and serves as an expert witness in cases involving human factors issues. He has executed or directed over 100 research and development contracts, subcontracts, and consulting activities. In addition, he has authored or coauthored over 90 technical reports, journal articles, and professional presentations. He received the Human Factors Society's Jack A. Kraft Award for his research on human factors issues in the mining industry. Dr. Sanders is a member of the Ergonomics Society and Society of Automotive Engineers. He is a fellow in the Human Factors Society and has served that organization as president, secretary-treasurer, and chair of the Education Committee and Educators Professional Group. Dr. Sanders is also a fellow of Division 21 (Division of Applied Experimental and Engineering Psychologists) of the American Psychological Association.

DR. ERNEST J. McCORMICK (deceased) was Professor Emeritus, Purdue University. His academic career as an industrial psychologist covered a span of 30 years at Purdue. His first edition of this text (then titled *Human Engineering*) was published in 1957. Dr. McCormick's other major publications include *Industrial and Organizational Psychology* (now in its eighth edition) and *Job Analysis: Methods and Applications*. He was responsible for development of the position analysis questionnaire (PAQ), a structured, computerized job analysis procedure being used by numerous organizations; he was president of PAQ Services, Inc. He has served on various advisory panels and committees, including the Army Scientific Advisory Panel, the Navy Advisory Board for Personnel Research, and the Committee on Occupational Classification and Analysis of the National Academy of Sciences. His awards include the Paul M. Fitts award of the Human Factors Society, the Franklin V. Taylor award of the Society of Engineering Psychologists, and the James McKeen Cattell award of the Society of Industrial and Organizational Psychology.

**Dedicated to the Memory of
Ernest J. McCormick**

CONTENTS

PREFACE   xi

PART 1   INTRODUCTION

1   Human Factors and Systems   3

2   Human Factors Research Methodologies   23

PART 2   INFORMATION INPUT

3   Information Input and Processing   47

4   Text, Graphics, Symbols, and Codes   91

5   Visual Displays of Dynamic Information   132

6   Auditory, Tactual, and Olfactory Displays   160

7   Speech Communications   197

PART 3   HUMAN OUTPUT AND CONTROL

8   Physical Work and Manual Materials Handling   225

9   Motor Skills   273

10   Human Control of Systems   301

11   **Controls and Data Entry Devices**   334

12   **Hand Tools and Devices**   383

PART 4   **WORKPLACE DESIGN**

13   **Applied Anthropometry, Work-Space Design,
and Seating**   415

14   **Arrangement of Components
within a Physical Space**   456

15   **Interpersonal Aspects of Workplace Design**   485

PART 5   **ENVIRONMENTAL CONDITIONS**

16   **Illumination**   511

17   **Climate**   551

18   **Noise**   589

19   **Motion**   622

PART 6   **HUMAN FACTORS APPLICATIONS**

20   **Human Error, Accidents, and Safety**   655

21   **Human Factors and the Automobile**   696

22   **Human Factors in Systems Design**   726

APPENDIXES

A   **List of Abbreviations**   759
B   **Control Devices**   764
C   **NIOSH Recommended Action Limit Formula
for Lifting Tasks**   769

INDEXES
  Name Index   771
  Subject Index   781

PREFACE

This book deals with the field of *human factors,* or *ergonomics,* as it is also called. In simple terms, the term *human factors* refers to *designing for human use.* Ten years ago, it would have been difficult to find very many people outside the human factors profession who could tell you what human factors or ergonomics was. Today, things are different. Human factors and ergonomics are in the news. Visual and somatic complaints of computer terminal users have been linked to poor human factors design. The incident at Three-Mile Island nuclear power station highlighted human factors deficiencies in the control room. The words *human factors* and especially *ergonomics* have also found their way into advertisements for automobiles, computer equipment, and even razors. The field is growing, as evidenced by the increase in the membership of human factors professional societies, in graduate programs in human factors, and in job opportunities.

We intended this book to be used as a textbook in upper-division and graduate-level human factors courses. We were also aware that this book has been an important resource for human factors professionals over the last six editions and 35 years. To balance these two purposes, we have emphasized the empirical research basis of human factors, we have stressed basic concepts and the human factors considerations involved in the topics covered, and we have supplied references for those who wish to delve into a particular area. We have tried to maintain a scholarly approach to the field. Unfortunately, there are times when our presentation may be a little technical or "dry," especially when we are presenting information that would be more appropriate for the practicing human factors specialist than for students. For this we apologize, but we hope the book will be one students will want to keep as a valuable reference.

For students, we have written a workbook to accompany this text (published by Kendall-Hunt Publishing Co., Dubuque, Iowa). Included in the workbook, for each chapter, are a list of key terms and self-contained projects that use concepts and information contained in this book.

There has been a virtual information explosion in the human factors field over the years. The first edition of this book, published in 1957, contained 16 chapters and 370 references. This edition contains 22 chapters and over 900 references. In 1972, the Human Factors Society (HFS) first published a proceedings of their annual meeting. It contained 106 papers and was 476 pages long. The proceedings for the 1991 HFS annual meeting contained over 350 papers and was 1600 pages long! In this book we have tried to cover both traditional and emerging areas of human factors, but it was impossible to include everything. The specific research material included in the text represents only a minute fraction of the vast amount that has been carried out in specific areas. It has been our interest to use as illustrative material examples of research that are relatively important or that adequately illustrate the central points in question. Although much of the specific material may not be forever remembered by the reader, we hope that the reader will at least develop a deep appreciation of the importance of considering human factors in the design of the features of the world in which we work and live. Appreciation is expressed to the many investigators whose research is cited. References to their work are included at the end of each chapter. To those investigators whose fine work we did not include, we apologize and trust they understand our predicament. We would also like to thank the following reviewers for their many helpful comments and suggestions: John G. Casali, Virginia Polytechnic Institute; Rick Gill, University of Idaho; Martin Helander, SUNY, Buffalo; John Lyman, University of California, Los Angeles; Joseph P. Meloy, Milwaukee School of Engineering; Edward J. Rinalducci, University of Central Florida; and William C. Howell, Rice University.

This edition represents some changes from the last edition. In addition to a general updating of the material (almost 30 percent of the figures are new), a new chapter on motor skills (Chapter 9) has been added. Several chapters have been extensively revised and renamed, including: Chapter 8, Physical Work and Manual Materials Handling; Chapter 20, Human Error, Accidents, and Safety; Chapter 4, Text, Graphics, Symbols, and Codes; and Chapter 13, Applied Anthropometry, Workspace Design, and Seating. We welcome comments and suggestions for making improvements in future editions.

It is with sadness that I report that Professor Ernest J. McCormick (Mac to his friends) died on February 9, 1990. Mac's passing came as we were starting to work on this edition of the book. I was deprived of a much admired colleague and a wonderful writing partner. His input and critiques are missing from this edition, but his contributions to the book over the last 35 years live on in every chapter. When I was a graduate student at Purdue University, twenty-odd years ago, I was asked to teach Mac's courses while he was in India. One of the perks was being allowed to use his office. I remember sitting in his chair for the first time. Although physically larger than Mac, I vividly recall feeling small sitting there. As I worked on this edition without Mac's help, I had a similar feeling. He has left an empty chair that will be hard to fill. Mac is survived by his wife Emily and two daughters Wynne and Jan. Mac was a model of professionalism and integrity. He was a person of quiet wit, keen analytic ability, and intellect. He will be missed.

Mark S. Sanders

HUMAN FACTORS IN ENGINEERING AND DESIGN

PART ONE

INTRODUCTION

1   Human Factors and Systems
2   Human Factors Research Methodologies

CHAPTER 1

HUMAN FACTORS AND SYSTEMS

In the bygone millennia our ancestors lived in an essentially "natural" environment in which their existence virtually depended on what they could do directly with their hands (as in obtaining food) and with their feet (as in chasing prey, getting to food sources, and escaping from predators). Over the centuries they developed simple tools and utensils, and they constructed shelter for themselves to aid in the process of keeping alive and making life more tolerable.

The human race has come a long way from the days of primitive life to the present with our tremendous array of products and facilities that have been made possible with current technology, including physical accoutrements and facilities that simply could not have been imagined by our ancestors in their wildest dreams. In many civilizations of our present world, the majority of the "things" people use are made by people. Even those engaged in activities close to nature—fishing, farming, camping—use many such devices.

The current interest in human factors arises from the fact that technological developments have focused attention (in some cases dramatically) on the need to consider human beings in such developments. Have you ever used a tool, device, appliance, or machine and said to yourself, "What a dumb way to design this; it is so hard to use! If only they had done this or that, using it would be so much easier." If you have had such experiences, you have already begun to think in terms of human factors considerations in the design of things people use. Norman (1988), in an entertaining book, provides numerous examples of everyday things that were not designed from a human factors perspective, including single-control shower faucets, videocassette recorders, and stove-top controls. In a sense, the goal of human factors is to guide the applications of technology in the direction of benefiting humanity. This text offers an overview of the human factors field; its various sections and chapters deal with some of the more important aspects of the field as they apply to such objectives.

HUMAN FACTORS DEFINED

Before attempting to define human factors, we should say a word about terms. *Human factors* is the term used in the United States and a few other countries. The term *ergonomics*, although used in the United States, is more prevalent in Europe and the rest of the world. Some people have tried to distinguish between the two, but we believe that any distinctions are arbitrary and that, for all practical purposes, the terms are synonymous. Another term that is occasionally seen (especially within the U.S. military) is *human engineering*. However, this term is less favored by the profession, and its use is waning. Finally, the term *engineering psychology* is used by some psychologists in the United States. Some have distinguished engineering psychology, as involving basic research on human capabilities and limitations, from human factors, which is more concerned with the *application* of the information to the design of things. Suffice it to say, not everyone would agree with such a distinction.

We approach the definition of human factors in terms of its focus, objectives, and approach.

Focus of Human Factors

Human factors focuses on human beings and their interaction with products, equipment, facilities, procedures, and environments used in work and everyday living. The emphasis is on human beings (as opposed to engineering, where the emphasis is more on strictly technical engineering considerations) and how the design of things influences people. Human factors, then, seeks to change the things people use and the environments in which they use these things to better match the capabilities, limitations, and needs of people.

Objectives of Human Factors

Human factors has two major objectives. The first is to enhance the effectiveness and efficiency with which work and other activities are carried out. Included here would be such things as increased convenience of use, reduced errors, and increased productivity. The second objective is to enhance certain desirable human values, including improved safety, reduced fatigue and stress, increased comfort, greater user acceptance, increased job satisfaction, and improved quality of life.

It may seem like a tall order to enhance all these varied objectives, but as Chapanis (1983) points out, two things help us. First, only a subset of the objectives are generally of highest importance in a specific application. Second, the objectives are usually correlated. For example, a machine or product that is